James Kennedy

Poems on Scottish and American Subjects

James Kennedy

Poems on Scottish and American Subjects

Reprint of the original, first published in 1883.

1st Edition 2024 | ISBN: 978-3-38533-169-3

Verlag (Publisher): Outlook Verlag GmbH, Zeilweg 44, 60439 Frankfurt, Deutschland
Vertretungsberechtigt (Authorized to represent): E. Roepke, Zeilweg 44, 60439 Frankfurt, Deutschland
Druck (Print): Books on Demand GmbH, In de Tarpen 42, 22848 Norderstedt, Deutschland

POEMS

ON

SCOTTISH AND AMERICAN SUBJECTS

JAMES KENNEDY.

SECOND EDITION.

NEW YORK: L. D. & J. A. ROBERTSON, 60 BARCLAY STREET.
EDINBURGH AND GLASGOW: JOHN MENZIES & CO.
LONDON: SIMPKIN, MARSHALL & CO.

.

PREFACE TO THE FIRST EDITION.

In submitting this volume of compositions in verse to the consideration of his countrymen in America and the lovers of Scottish literature, the author takes the opportunity of stating to his many friends who have from time to time suggested to him the propriety of publishing a collection of his productions in verse, that the apparent delay in not issuing such publication at an earlier date is not to be attributed to any fear of a lack of a proper appreciation and patronage of such work, but from the fact that in looking over the material in hand the author had doubts as to whether much that had been written almost extemporaneously and on subjects of ephemeral interest were suitable for the more permanent position which a collection in book-form implies.

The author has therefore endeavored to select only such pieces as would likely be of interest to the general reader, to whom he might further state that the chief object of these productions have been to reflect in some measure the feelings and experiences of the Scot in America. The author feels in common with all who have gone to a far country, that the love of our native land, like all loves, becomes more impassioned when separated from its object. He feels that time and distance only intensify the feeling, and the dear old land becomes more glorified, as mountains gather azure from distance. This feeling is not akin to one of discontent in the land of our adoption, enjoying as we do so much of the bountiful blessings of Providence, together with all that is highest and best in the acquired wisdom of the ages.

We feel that neither absence nor interest nor new affec
tions can take us wholly from our fatherland, but that, whether-
we will or not, part of our spirit still seems to linger among
the fair scenes of Caledonia. These, vivified by the memories
of human associations that crowd upon us, come like the
remembrance of lost but unforgotten loves, lending a sad,
sweet pleasure to our lives, and these have been the main
influences that have called into vocal utterance much that
the author presents in this volume.

It has not been, however, the single object of keeping green
the memories of the fatherland that has acted as the only
motive in the author's mind. He looks upon the stories of the
lives and fortunes of the people who leave Scotland and seek
their fortunes in America as being peculiarly suited for imagi-
native treatment. There are no people more heroic. In the
battle of life the burden of labor sits light upon them. They
are self-reliant, and hence are marked by strong individuality,
which gives rise to incident, which kindles imagination.

That the author has not reached his ideal will only be too
apparent, the only serious attempt being in "The Southron
Cavalier," where he has endeavored to throw an air of chival-
ric romance around the career of a young Scot in America.
This composition, although written with much care, he presents with much diffidence. He might claim that to him the
Scottish dialect is the language of his heart, but he offers no
excuse for attempting to write in English. If the author does
not show a knowledge of English composition, it is because
he has not taken full advantage of the educational facilities
which America offers to the young men whose early opportu-
nities for learning may have been limited.

To those of his countrymen and others, many of whom are among the most distinguished citizens of America, who have done the author the kindness to order copies of the book in advance of its publication, he can only assure them that whatever little pleasure the perusal of its contents may afford them, it cannot equal the rare pleasure their encouragement has given him. The kind words that have come to him from near and far have already almost dispelled that diffidence which naturally arises in the mind in appearing in a new light before the public ; and he feels already, that having the approbation of those whom he esteems the most, he stands surrounded as by a phalanx, and the neglect of the indifferent or the aspersions of the fault-finding critic cannot greatly disturb him.

NEW YORK, March 24th, 1883.

NOTE TO THE SECOND EDITION.

IN issuing a second edition the Author desires to express his gratitude for the warm interest manifested by his friends and countrymen in the work. But for their generous aid such rapid disposal of the first issue could not have been made.

The Author had hoped that in the event of a second edition he would have taken the opportunity to add other compositions in verse to the volume, but he has not had time to finish any unpublished composition on hand, or collect other fugitive pieces worthy of a place in the volume. The book, however, already contains the best the Author has to offer, and perhaps it is better to remain as it is.

NEW YORK, May 1st, 1883.

CONTENTS.

CHARACTER SKETCHES, ETC.—

MISCELLANEOUS POEMS.

TO MY NATIVE LAND.

CALEDONIA!—brightest. rarest
    Gem that shin'st on earth or sea :
Lover-like, forever fairest
    Fancy paints thy charms to me.

Day by day thy mem'ries haunt me.
    Rich in all things bright and rare :
Night by night sweet dreams enchant me
    Of thy beauties fresh and fair :

And my spirit seems to wander,
    Ever joyous, fond and free,
O'er thy hills whose purple grandeur
    Glows in king-like majesty :

Through thy glens that sweetly nourish
    Many a flower of bonnie bloom,
Where the spinks and blue-bells flourish
    Bright among the brier's perfume ;

Where the rowans hang like lustres
    Red within the shady dells;
And the sweet blaeberry clusters
    Blue among the heather-bells;

Where the laverock and the lintie
    Sing their lilts o' pure delight:
And the robin whistles canty
    To the warbling yellow-yite:

Where the deeds o' martial glory
    Hallow ilka hill and dale;
Where the wild, romantic story
    Casts its charm o'er ilka vale:

Where sweet Poesy pipes her numbers
    Till the minstrels' airy dream
Haunts the wild where Echo slumbers,
    Sings in ilka crystal stream:

Where true manhood dwells serenely
    Moulded in heroic grace,
And fair virtue, meek but queenly
    Beams in woman's angel face.

Thus to me thy memory giveth
    Joys that sweeten life's dull care;
Thus with me thy beauty liveth
    Like a presence ev'rywhere.

And the years that pass but brighten
 All thy graces fair and free,
As the moon-lit waters whiten
 On the dim and distant sea.

So may thou dwell with me ever
 Through the ceaseless flow of years,
Till the deep and dark Forever
 Ends my earthly hopes and fears.

Then 't were happy, CALEDONIA,
 Aye to dwell serene in you.
Aye among the blythe and bonnie,
 Aye among the tried and true.

TO THE HUMMING BIRD.

Braw birdie, when in brambly howes,
Whaur mony a buss entangled grows,
And bonnie flow'rs in beauty spring,
I've seen thee fauld thy quivering wing,
While rapt I stood, amazed to see
The glowing hues that gleamed on thee—
The red, the blue, the gowd, the green,
The pearly gloss, the siller sheen;
Then quick ere yet the eager eye
Had half perceived each dazzling dye,
Awa' ye fluttered frae the sight,
Like fire-flaucht in the cloud o' night.

Sic like 's when in the day's dull thrang
Time drags the weary hours alang;
Bright fancy flashes on the mind
Some bonnie blink o' wondrous kind—
Wild glens wi' burnies bick'rin doun,
Far frae the stoury, noisy toun;
Green woods an' sweet secluded dells,
Whaur silence aye serenely dwells;
Fond faces—rare auld warks an' ways
That graced the light o' ither days—
Come sudden on th' enraptured view,
Then vanish in a blink—like you.

But speed thee on thy fairy flight,
Whaur sweetest blossoms tempt thy sight;
An' round thee may ilk gladsome thing
Light as the flaffer o' thy wing
Aye keep thee blythe, nor aught e'er mar
The bonnie, braw, wee thing ye are.
Owrejoyed am I when happy chance
But brings thee in a passing glance.

Thus come, O Poesy! grace divine!
Come wi' that kindling fire o' thine,
That lends the dull imaginings
The beauties of a thousand things;
And though thy flashing fancies flit,
Like this wee birdie's restless fit,
Thy briefest glint shall grandly glow
As bright as Iris' radiant bow.

AULD SCOTIA IN THE FIELD.

'Twas summer, and green earth's fair face
    Was wreathed in vernal bloom;
Each dewy flow'ret lent its grace
    And shed its sweet perfume.

The bright birds in the shady groves,
    On ev'ry bush and tree,
Sang sweetly to their list'ning loves
    Their songs of melody.

And from the city's busy throng
    Went forth a joyous band,
To swell the universal song
    That echoed through the land.

And deep within a shady wood
    Joy held its sylvan court;
And thither thronged the multitude
    To witness manly sport.

Again we joyed to sally forth
    In tartan's plumed array;
Wild music of our native North,
    Inspiring, led the way;

And Scottish banners waved above
  The heads of Scottish men,
As if the Pennsylvanian grove
  Were Caledonian glen.

Nor wanted there as brawny arms
  As erst in days of yore
Were nobly raised in war's alarms
  For old green Albyn's shore,

And won that glory which has given
  A halo brightly thrown
Around her as a gleam from heaven—
  A glory all her own.

And mem'ries thronged till bright there seem'd
  Beneath fair Freedom's sun—
Columbia's—Scotia's lustre gleam'd,
  And spread their lights in one.

Thus ever may they seem to shine,
  Homes of the brave and free,
Upholding manhood's right divine
  Of God-like liberty ;

And buoyant on the wings of fame,
  Till Nature's destined plan
In thunder voices loud proclaim
  The brotherhood of man.

ADDRESS TO THE MOSQUITOES.

Lang-nebbit, bizzin, bitin' wretches,
That fire my skin wi' blobs an' splatches ;
Till vex'd wi' yeukie claws an' scratches,
       I think I'm free
To say the warld has seen few matches
        To Job an' me.

Sae aft you've gar't me fret an' fume,
My vera spirit ye consume
Wi' everlasting martyrdom—
       Ye wicked tartars,
You've surely settled on my room
       For your headquarters!

Asleep or wauken, air or late,
Like Nick himsel' ye are na blate ;
But like the doom o' pendin' fate
       Aboon my head,
Ye keep me in a waefu' state
       O' quakin' dread.

Whiles like a fury I've been stan'in',
An' clos'd my mou to keep frae bannin,
Whiles some destructive scheme I'm plannin'
       Your race to scatter—
O could I ram ye in a cannon,
       An' then lat blatter!

When pensive in my fav'rite neuk,
I glow'r owre some auld-farrant beuk,
Like leeches then my bluid ye sook,
    Then bizz and flee;
An' then begins th' infernal yeuk
    That angers me.

When lost in mazy contemplation
And soars supreme imagination,
How aft on fancy's fair creation
    The curtain draps:
Ye bizz, an' blinks o' inspiration
    At ance collapse!

O would some towsie-headed tyke,
Wha strives to make some new bit **fyke**,
Invent a plan to sweep your byke
    Frae human dwallins,
I'd sing his praise as heigh's ye like
    In braw, braid ballan's.

But fix'd ye are 'mang human ills—
Whose bitter cup your bitin' fills;
Nor auld wives' cures nor doctors' bills
    Can mend the case—
Firm as the everlasting hills
    Ye keep your place.

But could I gain some grace or ither,
To teach me in ilk warslin swither,
To tak the guid an' ill thegither
      Without complaint,
Then might we dwell wi' ane anither
      In calm content.

But sae it is,—ye maun hae food,
An' I maun guard my ain heart's bluid;
But could ye scrape a livelihood
      Some ither where.
I would be yours in gratitude
      For evermair.

WHISKY'S AWA'!

What news is this? I speer fu' fain,
Is this some joke o' th' printer's ain?
Na faith, it's truth that he's been say'n':
      They've pass'd a law
Through Pennsylvania, dale an' plain—
      Whisky's awa'!

Weel might a pride light ilka eye,
An' ilk ane haud their head fu' high,
An' celebrate their Fourth July
      Wi' mirth an' a',
An' roar o' cannon, rend the sky—
      Whisky's awa'!

Lang has it been your pridefu' boast,
What time the tyrant British host
Departed, like a frighted ghost,
   At Freedom's craw :
A deadlier fae has left your coast -
   Whisky's awa' !

Nae mair the drunkard's raggit bairns,
Like misers, live on scraps an' parin's,
An' gloomy jails, whase rusty airns
   Fulfill the law,
May tumble down in shapeless cairns—
   Whisky's awa' !

Good Templars now, an' bad anes baith,
May cast aside their glitt'rin' graith;
Nor need they paint vile whisky's scaith
   As black's a craw,
Nor sign the pledge, nor tak the aith—
   Whisky's awa' !

Rejoice ilk mither—sorrow now
Need never cloud your anxious brow.
Ye lasses, when ye mak your vow,
   Let hopes ne'er fa'—
Your lads, like steel, will aye stand true—
   Whisky's awa' !

If sultry weather should prevail,
To slocken drouth nae ane need fail:
There's caller cronk an' ginger ale,
      Or, best o' a',
In Susquehanna dip your pail—
      Whisky's awa'!

O caller water! gowd or gear
Compared wi' thee maun tak the rear;
Thou never garr'd the bitter tear
      O' mis'ry fa'!
Pure be thy fountain evermair—
      Whisky's awa'!

Now Peace, wi' Plenty on its wing,
Contentment's sweets may swiftly bring,
An' Truth stand up, an' Virtue spring
      As pure as snaw!
While Universal Joy doth sing,
      Whisky's awa'!

NORAN WATER: AN IDYL.

I stood where Erie's waters flow
    O'er steep Niag'ra's awful brink,
And watch'd where to the depths below
    The mighty torrents fold and sink;
And as my senses seemed to swim,
    And quicker beat my throbbing heart,
The sounding waters sang their hymn,
    More grand than music's measured art.

And I have sailed upon the flood
    That lave's Manhattan's busy shore,
By tangled brake and dark-green wood,—
    By beetling crags moss-grown and hoar,—
By cultured fields where graceful bends
    The maize's yellow-crested stalk:
And where, to swell her tide, descends
    The waters of the dark Mohawk.

And I have gazed with joy untold
    Where through Wyoming's valley green
The noble Susquehanna roll'd
    In stately majesty serene:
While pure as that unclouded day,
    Far seen in azure skies profound,
The magic of a poet's lay
    Made all the scene seem hallowed ground.

But these, though happy thoughts they bring,
    When clear upon the memory's eye
They glow in bright imagining
    As vivid as reality;
Yet dearer memories fondly forth
    Come linked with Noran's crystal stream,
That, bright as in its native North,
    Oft sparkles in my fancy's dream.

O Noran! how I see thee dance
    By heath-clad hills alone, unseen,
Save where the lonely eagle's glance
    Surveys thee from his crag serene.
Forever joyous thou dost seem,
    Still sportive as a child at play,
Who, lost in pleasure's careless dream,
    Makes merry music all the day.

By fairy nooks I see thee flow,
    Nor pausing in thy artless song
Till where the fir trees spreading low
    Obscure thy stream their arms among.
There, sweet amid the shady gloom,
    Thou hear'st the blackbird chant his lay,
Thou see'st the pale primroses bloom,
    And silent ling'rest on thy way!

Then forth thy waters dazzling come
    Where sweet-brier scents the balmy breeze,
And where the wild bees softly hum
    Faint echo of thy harmonies.
Green spiky gorse thy banks adorn,
    Gold-tassell'd broom thy fringe-work weave,
While feathered choirs from dewy morn
    Make melody till dewy eve.

Then, foaming in fantastic flakes,
    Thou dashest down a deep ravine,
Where overhanging wild-wood makes
    A canopy of leafy green.
While sweet as when cathedral naves
    Are filled with voices grave and gay,
Soft echoes from their hidden caves
    Repeat thy ringing roundelay.

Then eddying deep by flowery dells,
    Or babbling on by clovery lea,
Thou glittering glid'st, while crystal bells
    Of diamond lustre dance on thee,
And happy children's eager eye
    Pursues them, or with tiny hands
Collect the pearly shells that lie
    Begemming bright thy silvery sands.

Then on by pleasant farms that breathe
    Of calm contentment's happy clime;
Or laughing where the ivy's wreath
    Clings round the ruins of olden time.
And on where stately mansions rise,
    Or lowly gleams the cottage hearth;
Unchanged thy smile still meets the skies,
    Unchanged still rings thy song of mirth.

Till like a maid whose bridal morn
    Beholds her decked to meet her love,
Thou com'st where gayest flowers adorn,
    And sweetest warblers charm the grove;
And mingling with the Esk's clear stream,
    In fond embrace he claspeth thee,
And smiling 'neath the sunny beam,
    Rolls grandly to the German Sea.

O Noran! bright thy memory brings
    My careless boyhood back to me,
When ardent hope on fancy's wings
    Beheld life's future gleam like thee.
But though life's path be dull and strange,
    And rare the promised joys I meet,
In thee I have, through time and change,
    One golden memory ever sweet!

WEE CHARLIE.

"I shall go to him, but he shall not return to me."—II Samuel, 12th c., 23d v.

O gin my heart could hae its wiss
    Within this weary warld o' care,
I'd ask nae glow o' balmy bliss
    To dwell around me evermair.
For joy were mine beyond compare,
    An' O how happy would I be,
If Heaven would grant my earnest prayer,
    An' bring wee Charlie back to me.

He cam' like sunshine when the buds
    Burst into blossoms sweet and gay,
He dwelt like sunshine when the cluds
    Are vanish'd frae the eye o' day.
He pass'd as daylight fades away,
    An' darkness spreads owre land an' sea:
Nae wonder though in grief I pray,
    O bring wee Charlie back to me.

When Pleasure brings her hollow joys,
    Or Mirth awakes at Friendship's ca',
Or Art her varied power employs
    To mak dull Time look blithe an' braw,
How feckless seem they ane an' a'
    When sad Remembrance dims my e'e,—
O tak thae idle joys awa'
    An' bring wee Charlie back to me.

But vain's the cry; he maunna cross
    Frae where he dwells in bliss unseen,
Nor need I mourn my waefu' loss,
    Nor muse on joys that might hae been.
When cauld death comes to close my een,
    Awa' beyond life's troublous sea,
In everlasting joy serene,
    They'll bring wee Charlie back to me.

TO THE SHADE OF BURNS,

ON THE OCCASION OF UNVEILING A STATUE TO HIS MEMORY
IN CENTRAL PARK, NEW YORK.

Bright spirit, whose transcendant song
    Hath charmed earth's utmost bound,
Till from her solitudes among
    Comes ringing back the sound.

Come where the wild Atlantic waves
    Have hush'd their ceaseless roar,
And, softly as a zephyr, laves
    Manhattan's busy shore.

See where the thronging thousands stand
    In reverence to thee:
The witching charm,—the magic wand,—
    Thy matchless minstrelsy!

They see in monumental bronze
    Thy manly form and face;
They hear in music's sweetest tones
    Thy spirit's grander grace.

And though from many lands they came,
    To brotherhood they've grown,
By thee their pulses throb the same,
    Their hearts are all thy own.

And we whose childhood's home was thine,
    What joy thy memory brings!
To us thou seem'st as more divine
    Than earth-created things.

For all youth's fairy scenes and glee,
    Loves, hopes and fancies fain,
In Poesy's art illumed by thee,
    Come back to us again :

And past and present all appear
    Transfigured by thy grace,
Till Hope points where in grander sphere
    We'll meet thee face to face.

ANGUS RANKIN'S ELEGY.

O brither Scots whaure'er ye be,
That lo'e auld Scotland's melodie,
Come join my wail wi' tearfu' e'e
   An' hearts that bleed,
An' sad an' lanely mourn wi' me
   For him that's dead!

Now silence haunts baith house an' ha'
Sin' Angus Rankin's worn awa';
He wha sae sweetly aye could blaw
   The tunefu' reed,
The sweetest minstrel o' them a'—
   Alas! he's dead!

O sirs! what glowing pictures thrang
In memory's treasured joys amang,
Whaur blythely aye his chanter rang,
   A tunefu' skreed,
In warbled numbers loud an' lang—
   But Rankin's dead!

How aft his sweet, inspiring strain
Wing'd Fancy owre the dark blue main,
Till heathery hill, an' grassy plain,
   An' daisied mead,
Came fresh on memory's e'e again—
   But Rankin's dead!

An' aft by some Columbian dell,
In woody grove or breezy fell.
His art divine threw sic a spell—
      It seemed indeed
The very grund was Scotland's sel'—
      But Rankin's dead!

When Hallowe'en or blithe New Year.
Or auld Saint Andrew's Day drew near,
His pipes aye roused sic social cheer—
      Fowk took nae heed.
But danc'd till they could hardly steer—
      But Rankin's dead!

When kilted Scots made grand parade,
In bonnets blue an' belted plaid,
Wi' what triumphant, martial tread
      He took the lead!
Heroic graces round him spread—
      But now he's dead!

Ilk clansman mark'd his manly air,
His modest mien an' form sae fair,
The eagle eye, the raven hair
      That graced his head:
Alas! he'll cheer their hearts nae mair—
      For Rankin's dead!

When athletes mustered on the green,
An' feats o' strength an' skill were seen,
What rousing blasts he blew between,
      An' pibroch's skreed!
He was th' Apollo o' the scene—
      But Rankin's dead!

When dancers danced the Highland Fling,
How Angus made the welkin ring!
Till tune an' time an' ilka thing
      Sae fired the head,
That nimble feet amaist took wing—
      But Rankin's dead!

Though fortune's wrang he whiles did bear it,
Nae spite nor envy gnawed his spirit;
But keen to praise another's merit
      An' wish them speed;
Rare gifts o' grace he did inherit—
      But Rankin's dead!

But weak's my muse to chant his praise,
Weel worthy o' mair lofty lays;
But in the light o' future days,
      Wi' pensive heed,
I'll muse upon the kindly ways
      O' him that's dead!

An' aft when some soul-stirring tune
Rings blithe as birds in joyfu' June,
I'll think his spirit frae abune
            Inspires the reed,
Or else my dancing days were dune
            Sin' Rankin's dead!

Come pipers, ye wha lo'ed him weel,
Come Cleland, famed for blithesome reel;
Come Grant an' Laurie, true as steel—
            An' Peter Reid,
Come blaw some weird an' wild fareweel
            For Angus dead!

Come Music frae thy starry sphere,
Come mourn thy loss amang us here,
Gar Fame gae sound her trumpet clear,
            Till a' tak' heed,
An' mournfu' drap a kindly tear
            For Rankin dead!

THE SOUTHRON CAVALIER:

A ROMANCE OF THE AMERICAN REBELLION.

INSCRIBED TO PROF. ALEX. J. C. SKENE, M.D., BROOKLYN.

CANTO THE FIRST.

I.

'T was evening, and a festal ball
　　Re-echoed with a joyous throng;
And Charleston held high carnival,
　　And merry dance and swelling song
Alternate did their powers prolong;
　　While Carolina's opal sky
Serenely glanced her stars among
　　Like sparkles of a laughing eye.

II.

And, stranger to that sunny land,
　　I reck'd not of the how or why;
Secession's rudely rampant hand
　　Seemed peaceful to my youthful eye,
For pleasure hailed its birth, and I,
　　All free as is the ambient air,
Responded, and a spirit high
　　Spread wildly joyous ev'rywhere.

III.

And beauty's circle saw me then
    Gay as a bird of wanton wing,
That lightly flits and comes again
    Rejoicing in the voice of Spring;
Nor sad note dulls its carolling,
    Nor grove alluring checks its flight;
But, buoyant as an airy thing,
    Still flutters in the eye of light.

IV.

'T was then amid the brilliant throng
    The sunlight of a beauteous face
Shone as a meteor shines among
    The planets in its fiery race;
And matchless mien and maiden grace
    Dwelt round a form so pure and fair,—
That there all beauty found a place,
    All rare perfections mingled there.

V.

We met, we mingled in the dance;
    And while she tripp'd on fairy feet,
Her artless words, her ev'ry glance
    Glowed innocently exquisite;
And swift did wingéd moments fleet
    Unnoticed, till like fading day,—
Ethereal,—evanescent,—sweet
    And lingeringly she passed away.

VI.

Then o'er my being stole that sense
    Which youth's prime passion only knows;
While fancy shadowing forth intense
    An ever-beauteous image throws
Athwart the soul, which comes and goes
    Like ripples on a lakelet's breast;
And breaks upon the mind's repose
    A joyless joy, a calm unrest.

VII.

But anxious days with fruitless schemes
    Brought not that peerless face again;
And weary nights and idle dreams
    Passed o'er me and my hopes in vain.
But, siren-like, fond fancy fain
    Lured expectation fondly forth,
Till like a frenzy in the brain
    All else were but as little worth.

VIII.

My life has been but as the stream
    Which dashes down the mountain side,
Nor lingereth it in soft sunbeam
    Nor shady forest waving wide,
Till where adown the vale doth glide
    Some gentle river calm and deep;
There the wild torrent curbs its pride,—
    There placidly it seems to sleep.

IX.

So paused my life's course, and the hours
　　Unheeded o'er me passed away
Till Spring-time with its wreath of flowers
　　Bloomed in the fragrant breath of May;
And Nature sang her roundelay
　　By woody wild and grassy grove;
And all was bright and pure and gay
　　And sweet as lovers' dreams of love.

X.

And from the busy city's throng
　　Went gaily forth a joyous band,
To swell the universal song
　　That echoed gladly through the land;
And manly sport ruled hand in hand
　　With varied pleasures' softer sway,
While swift-wing'd joy with magic wand
　　Soon sped our happy holiday.

XI.

And evening came—the golden hour
　　When earth seems meet for purer things
Than man, self-lost in pride of power,
　　Or tossed on vain imaginings.
Then soared my soul on buoyant wings
　　When wandering through the sylvan shades,
All silent save the murmurings
　　Of brooklets babbling down the glades.

XII.

The dark'ning twilight's silvery haze
    Hung dream-like round the distant woods;
The sinking sun with sapphire blaze
    Lit up the higher solitudes.
E'en still my fancy fondly broods
    O'er all the oft-remembered scene
That rose o'er all my darker moods
    As radiant rainbows rise serene.

XIII.

For in the leafy brake's embrace
    There stood love's fondly cherish'd dream
In sudden form, and face to face
    The idol of my life did seem
Bright as the star whose guiding gleam
    The wearied mariner's watchful eyes
Have found amid the wild extreme
    Of surging seas and scowling skies.

XIV.

But ne'er can tongue in words express
    Th' ecstatic joy—the fervid flame—
The awe that check'd each fond excess,
    As if seraphic-like she came;
While ev'ry feeling seem'd to frame
    Due homage to a thing divine,
And all around me breath'd the same
    As if great Nature's heart was mine.

XV.

A moment her ethereal eyes
    Beamed on me with their lustre bright,
While dear remembrance—coy surprise
    Gleam'd sweetly through like light on light,
Then quench'd their fire, as stars at night
    Are lost in cloudlets,—pure as in
The marble statue's eyelid's white
    That seem to veil a god within.

XVI.

But in that glance methought I read
    A kindred feeling fond and true,—
A young heart's yearning, fancy-fed,
    Where maiden love in silence grew;
And though she spoke not, fancy drew
    A sweeter language from those eyes
Than happy lover ever knew
    From lover's ruby lips to rise.

XVII.

Impassioned were the words that breathed
    My sudden transport swelling high;
While tender as the leaves that wreathed
    Around her were each low reply;
That, modest as the downcast eye,
    But half revealed the burning beam
That glowed in softest sympathy
    Ineffable as youth's fond dream.

XVIII.

But needless were it to relate
    Each heavenly joy my heart then knew,
When from my ravish'd soul elate
    The long, dull, darken'd night withdrew,
And love's celestial sun shone through,
    More bright than aught my hopes had known,
For earth seemed tinged with heaven's own hue,
    And all I loved seemed all my own.

XIX.

Swift-wingéd moments,—transport lost,—
    How soon—too soon ye passed away!
And left me, wildly tempest-tossed,
    To ev'ry varying thought a prey.
Ye sweetly shone as doth the ray
    Whose brief illusion mocks in vain
The darkness of an April day,
    When gathering clouds grow dark again.

XX.

For on our joy rude voices broke
    Tumultuous as a stormy sea;
An angry father fuming spoke,
    An irate lover frown'd on me
And breath'd of vengeance, as if he
    Some sudden, ruinous wrong had known.
In vain I spoke, and vainly she
    Wept as they left me all alone,—

XXI.

Lone as the wretch whose dungeon walls
 Are broken by some sudden might,
And hears a cheering voice that calls
 Him forth to freedom and to light:
When scarce o'er his enraptured sight
 The bright earth's glowing glories rise:
When sudden horrors 'whelm him quite,
 And double darkness seals his eyes.

XXII.

But 't was not mine to idly pine,
 Though favoring fortune seem'd afar.
I knew her heart was wholly mine,
 And hope, that shineth as a star
Through skies that overclouded are,
 Beam'd brightly still; and life's strange course
Glides fitly on, while every bar
 Oft seemeth but a quickening source.

XXIII.

And mine was quickened, and my heart
 Beat with the daring fire that warms
To higher things each nobler part;
 And when war's rudely wild alarms
Had roused the fiery South to arms
 A gleam shot through fate's frowning sky,
Bright as the breaking beam that charms
 The dull earth, like an open'd eye.

XXIV.

I stood within the long-sought home
  Of her I loved so fond and true.
Not as her father's guest I'd come;
  Nor wayward, rudely breaking through
His sovereign will; but well I knew
  If e'er I hoped with deeds to show
A heart where noble virtues grew,
  Occasion loudly bade me go.

XXV.

For stern as death a summons went
  To call fair Clara's father forth
To join the ranks the city sent
  To battle with th' invading North.
And youth's fond fire and valor's worth
  Self-sacrificing burned in me;
And feelings that from love have birth
  Soon blossom to maturity.

XXVI.

I told him how I loved his child—
  How for her sake I chose to go
And meet war's rugged dangers wild,
  That she, sweet soul, might never know
The anxious care, the tearful woe
  That mourns an absent father lost
In conflict with the furious foe
  Amid the deep ensanguined host.

XXVII.

Amazed, he utter'd not reply;
    Strange silence sealed his lips as though
A frowning cloud broke in the sky,
    And lurid lightning flash'd below
While crashing thunders come and go.
    So broke I—sudden—sullen—lone:
So flash'd my fiery purpose so,
    And—thunder-like—spoke, and was gone.

XXVIII.

Gone—mingling in the martial hum
    Of mustering armies,—vainly proud;
Gone where the rolling of the drum
    Was silenced 'neath the battle cloud,
Where rang tumultuous clamors loud,
    While deep-dyed slaughter spreading o'er,
Swathed in a universal shroud
    The conquered and the conqueror.

CANTO THE SECOND.

I.

While she,—the loved,—in aftertime
    I only learn'd with sad surprise,
That with the ardor of her clime,
    That burns beneath the Southern skies,
Ere friend or lover might surmise,
    She, passion-driven or hate-inspired,
Evanish'd from their watchful eyes,—
    Fair innocency frenzy-fired.

II.

Nor knew they how, nor wist they where,—
    Her hopes, her fears alike unknown,
Fled as a wild-bird wing'd in air
    That from its gilded cage has flown.
Nor had her mystery clearer grown
    When round the year's revolving time
Brought summer back, and, battle-blown,
    I stood in Pennsylvania's clime.

III.

Fair land, when thy ambrosial glades
    And wooded hills first met my eyes,
September's breath had touch'd thy shades
    With all the rainbow's varied dyes.
On memory's page fair scenes arise
    Where Nature's beauties all combine;
But 'neath thy bright autumnal skies,
    I know no scenes o'ermatching thine.

Thy hills though not like Alpine steep,
    Crown'd with its everlasting snows,
Thy cliffs hang o'er no foaming deep,
    Yet fairer beauties they disclose;
Hush'd solitude enchantment throws
    Around each fair, romantic scene,
And the enraptured spirit grows
    In soft resemblance, all serene.

V.

From blood-stained fields of war we came,
    A furious and a desp'rate band,
To spread destruction's wasting flame
    Impetuous o'er the peaceful land.
We smote with unrelenting hand;
    Ours was the roving, plundering horde
That heeds no voice but war's command,
    Makes no dispute but with the sword.

VI.

And on Virginia's war-worn soil
    Had triumph crown'd our conquering arms;
And days of battle, nights of toil
    Inured us to the rude alarms
That dim the sheen of glory's charms
    And petrify the soldier's heart,
Till kindly pity never warms
    Each feeling fix'd as sculptured art.

VII.

The glowing sun sank softly down.
    We reach'd the summit of a hill
That overlook'd a little town,
    And murmurs like a distant rill
Fell on the ear; all else was still,
    Save where at times the answering neigh
Of war-steeds echoed loud and shrill,
    Like wild war's ringing reveille.

VIII.

I linger'd, though I knew not why;
    The scene was placid, soft and fair,
And golden clouds hung in the sky,
    And dreamy stillness filled the air.
A mellow richness ev'rywhere
    Spread lavish to the longing gaze;
And fancy wander'd here and there
    Calm as the twilight's gathering haze.

IX.

Afar two streamlets seem'd to glide,
  With little space of woods between,
And then, diverging, seem'd to hide
  Their channels in the thick'ning green ;
Again emerging each was seen
  Approaching where in fond embrace
They met, and flowing on serene
  Sought Ocean for their resting place.

X.

And hope illum'd by fancy's ray,
  While mem'ry shadow'd forth the past,
In tone prophetic seem'd to say—
  Thus will the shades that overcast
Thy hapless love dispel at last ;
  And like the streamlets flowing free
Adown life's vale united fast
  Glide on toward eternity.

XI.

O could we know how vain the dreams
  Imagination fondly paints !
The hollowness that glitt'ring gleams
  Around the future's grand events ;
The balm that soothes our discontents,
  The hope that bids us bravely bear,
Are oft but fitful, frail restraints
  That keep us from a dull despair.

XII.

How oft when hope's serenest skies
    O'er life's dim pathway seems to spread,
Unseen some sullen storm-clouds rise
    And break disastrous overhead;
And where the mind's eye,—fancy fed.
    Beheld the future's shining path,
Stern truth but sees in awful dread
    Sad traces of the tempest's wrath.

XIII.

So was it as I idly dreamed,
    And o'er and o'er that landscape viewed;
While soul and sylvan beauty seemed
    To one incorporate same subdued;
A ruthless hand, that had pursued
    Through weary days my hapless life,
Hung vengeful o'er me,—hate-imbued,
    By baffled love,—to mortal strife.

XIV.

And sudden there a bolt of death
    From that stern hand had stunn'd my brain
And nearly stayed my ebbing breath;-
    I, swooning, fell in piercing pain,
My hand relaxed the bridle rein,
    A dizzy stupor o'er each sense
Rush'd flood-like, as the angry main
    Sweeps o'er the lone wreck's impotence.

XV.

And when again my wearied eyes
  With light relumed went wandering wide,
They fell not on the earth and skies
  Arrayed in autumn's golden pride:
A gray-haired senior by my side
  Bent with his kind face on me turned;
Indistinct shadows seemed to glide,
  A flick'ring taper faintly burned.

XVI.

Full oft through weary days that face
  Beam'd like an angel's, kind and sweet,
And gave my sorrow ev'n a grace
  All-delicately exquisite.
As when the wintry sunbeams greet
  In brighten'd radiance, sparkling free,
Where late the storm tempestuous beat
  With sudden force all furiously.

XVII.

He too had spent life's early days
  By Caledonia's wooded wild;
And lov'd to tell her storied praise
  And old romances grandly piled;
Enthusiastic as a child,
  His sympathetic soul would glow
With all the fire that wont to gild
  Chivalrous spirits long ago.

In all with reverent eye he saw
    The hands omnipotent that guide
The universe by certain law
    Where Destiny and Fate preside;
And all the ever-jarring tide
    Of conflict, he but deemed the springs
Whose purifying powers divide
    The golden truth from grosser things.

XIX.

He, skilfully, would venture o'er
    Discussion's sea where tempest-tossed
Frail barks on venturing from the shore
    Were oft in wild opinion lost:
Not his the blustering braggart's boast,
    But gathering wisdom from the past,
Portrayed with master skill the coast
    And peaceful havens reach'd at last.

XX.

Still gathering fervor as he passed
    From point to point, he wisely brought
Premises to conclusions fast
    That proud Oppression's power is nought:
Her conquests ever dearly bought
    Were fleeting as a passing breath,
While Freedom's arm triumphant fought
    And won an everlasting wreath.

XXI.

Discoursing thus, days rolled apace
    Till Spring-time with its wreath of flowers
Clasped Nature in her fond embrace,
    And decked again the sylvan bowers,
Where pensive oft the silent hours
    Would find me musing sad and strange,
Contemplating the varied powers
    That bring the slow result of change.

XXII.

The autumn leaves lay damp and dead
    Around the freshly budding stem;
And in my heart and in my head
    A ray of sad resemblance came:
As withered leaves, so hopes like them
    Lay strewn bedewed with silent tears;
While new ideas seemed to frame
    Fresh prospects for the coming years.

XXIII.

Still here and there to boughs there clung
    Some leaves, nor stormy winter's blast
Nor Time's decay had earthward wrung,—
    Sad relics of a blooming past:
Like them, all lifeless, clinging fast
    To me were thoughts of that sweet face,
Which, like a far-off beacon, cast
    A radiance through the darkening space.

XXIV.

I loved her still, but death-like cold
 And statue-like my love had grown.
No gilded future then could hold
 My idle fancy all its own.
Illusions one by one had flown
 Till resignation calmly viewed
Each vanish'd hope my heart had known
 Like youth's fond dreams by age subdued.

XXV.

But when successive gales have torn
 A lonely tree, and Summer's bloom
Sees but a wither'd trunk forlorn
 And leafless cast a saddening gloom;
As pitying misfortune's doom
 Mayhap the ivy's clustering wreath
Twines round it fresh as honor's plume
 Upon the barren brows of death.

XXVI.

So round my wither'd hopes there grew,
 Fresh as the ivy's rustling leaves,
A faith in Freedom strong and true
 Wherein prophetic fancy weaves
A golden future which receives
 In simple trust kind Nature's plan,
When long-obstructed truth achieves
 The common brotherhood of man.

XXVII.

Then those rude dangers I had braved
    Seem'd in my new-form'd faith to be
Vain efforts that a race enslaved,
    Whose heav'n-born right was to be free,
Might taste not of sweet liberty,
    And, feeling as the guilty feel,
I cast my former self from me
    With all a convert's fiery zeal.

XXVIII.

And Summer saw th' embattled field
    Receive me in its ranks again;
Not bold Secession's sword to wield
    Upholding Slavery's cursed reign,
But leagued for Union, to maintain
    That sacred shrine of Liberty;
And break Oppression's galling chain
    And set the gladden'd captive free.

CANTO THE THIRD.

I.

Again the tide of battle flowed
    Through Pennsylvania's peaceful land;
And Southron arms victorious glowed
    In wild Rebellion's daring hand.
Then Valor's fires were fiercely fanned;
    Then sent the North from near and far
In haste full many a loyal band
    Embattled in the ranks of war.

II.

And when the crash of conflict came
    The dawn beheld us where afar
We watch'd where smoke and bursting flame
    Gave signal of the open'd war.
Loud rang the wild discordant jar,
    Bright shone the moving flash of arms;
While Carnage drove her crimson car
    In fury 'mid the wild alarms.

III.

The Southrons charge—a wave of fire!
    The Northerns stand—a wall of steel!
Harsh swells the awful tumult, higher
    Than echoing thunder's lengthened peal!
Backward the charging columns reel
    As waves that from an angry main
Strike rocky shores, then shatter'd wheel
    In broken fragments back again.

IV.

And scarce had closed the fierce attack
    When sudden hands on me were laid;
Some Southron soldiers dragg'd me back
    A vilely-branded renegade.
Nor Law's strong arm was then delayed
    And Pity prayed nor for delay;
Force held me fast while Judgment said
    Next morn would be my dying day.

V.

Alone within the guarded tent
    I waited for the hour of doom,
While ghost-like memories came and went
    Like sad-eyed mourners round a tomb,
And far-off fancies' faded bloom
    Lit up the sad sepulchral show,
As when at evening's gathering gloom
    The distant cloudlets faintly glow.

VI.

And her I loved supreme o er all
    Seemed present with me, though unseen.
Her spirit held me as a thrall
    As if her slave my soul had been.
And does she mark this closing scene?
    I questioned, in my mute despair.
And does her soul from realms serene
    Come joyously to guide me there?

VII.

While thus my fancy fain had shaped
    The bright dawn of an endless day,
A saint-like figure darkly-draped
    In silence enter'd where I lay;
An angel seem'd she whose sad way,
    Self-sought where blew war's deadliest breath,
Oft led where, sweet as cheering ray,
    She smooth'd the dreary path of death.

VIII.

I gazed, and on me flash'd the light
    Of those bright eyes I deemed divine!
A death-like pallor—marble-white,
    Crept o'er each feature's fixéd line.
Then sank she in those arms of mine,
    So pale, so pure, so calmly fair,—
All perfect beauty seemed to shine
    In soft angelic sorrow there!

IX.

Anon she spoke in wild surprise,—
    Now joy would flush her pallid cheek,—
Now tears would dim her kindling eyes
    And tell the grief no tongue could speak.
Anon she conversed calm and meek,
    And oft our mutual sorrow broke,
Till brightly as a dawning streak
    A subtle, hopeful scheme she spoke.

X.

She bade me wrap me in her cloak,
    And, fearless, forth to freedom go,
And so disguised escape the stroke
    Of fate's last sad impending blow;
While she, assured that none would know
    Until all danger I had passed,
Would stay for me and gladly show
    That love triumphant is at last.

XI.

Brief words,—tear-moving, fond farewells
    Half-breath'd when hope to being springs
Mark moments that forever dwells
    Bright in the mind's rememberings.
Fears, hopes and joys, a thousand things,
    Seemed centred in the strange event;
I moved as if on airy wings
    As past the serried lines I went.

XII.

But peace went with me, and I sought
  Fair freedom where the banners rolled
O'er armies that for freedom fought
  Beneath that bright flag's starry fold
Whose blended crimson, blue and gold,
  Seemed to my wistful, hopeful eyes
Fair as the radiant bow of old
  That promised earth serener skies.

XIII.

And Clara came, and joy was there,
  While love and freedom unconfined
Glowed as the sunlight beaming fair
  On some shrunk plant of tender kind
That feels through all its sickly rind
  The influence of the genial glow;
So flood-like on my ravish'd mind
  Joy banish'd all my former woe.

XIV.

And care and sorrow fled away
  As if their presence ne'er had been
My sole companions night and day
  Through many a change of chme and s
O bright the heavens shine serene
  When stormy tempests wrath have pass
But brighter 't is when hope has see
  A full fruition come at last.

XV.

And glad the welcome we received
    At that calm Pennsylvanian vale,
Where dwelt the friend whose aid relieved
    My sorrow when misfortune's gale
Had tossed me as a shatter'd sail
    By sudden tempests rudely blown,
When wearied mariners gladly hail
    The shelter of a shore unknown.

XVI.

There dwell we happy and serene
    By summer woods and babbling streams,
The woodlands clad in leafy green,
    The waters glistening in the gleams
Of brightest iridescent beams.
    So fair, so grand seems earth and air
Surpassing all fond fancy's dreams,
    For love, bright love breathes ev'rywhere.

XVII.

At dawn,—soon as the rosy hue
    Of morning streaks the azure hills,
We wander forth while spangling dew
    Gleams on the golden daffodils;
Where sweet the flowery meadow fills
    Fresh incense to the new-born day,
While softly to the murmuring rills
    The song-bird sings his matin lay.

XVIII.

When bright the sun shines overhead
  We linger where the cedar trees
Their dark umbrageous shadows spread,
  While blending with the whispering breeze,
The song of birds, the hum of bees,
  The ceaseless rush of tiny wings
Harmonious ring like melodies
  That dwell in rapt rememberings.

XIX.

At evening when the silver moon
  Bathes hill and vale in liquid white,
And stars shine as in skies of June
  That seem scarce conscious of the night,
We sit enraptured with the sight,
  Our fancies fed on thoughts sublime,
And drink the joys of pure delight
  In golden hours in happy clime.

XX.

Nor deem we in our blissful state,
  While speed these summer days away,
That changing time or froward fate
  Can mar our joys with dull decay;
But love's links woven day by day
  Shine bright through years that are to be,
So Hymen gilds with golden ray
  Our path through fair futurity.

SONGS.

THE BONNIE LASS THAT'S FAR AWA'.

She's far awa' that won my heart,
    The lassie wi' the glancing een;
Nor Nature's wark, nor mortal's airt,
    Can bring me aught sae rare I ween;
For though the seas row deep between,
    An' lanely looks baith house an' ha',
Fond recollection aye keeps green
    The bonnie lass that's far awa'.

II.

Or if at times frae mem'ry's e'e
    She fades as gloaming fades to night,
If but some winsome lass I see,
    Wi' jimpy waist an' een that's bright,
My heart gaes fluttering at the sight,
    An' staps the breath I'm gaun to draw,
While fancy paints in glowing light
    The bonnie lass that's far awa'.

III.

Glide by, ye weary winter days;
    Glide by, ye nights sae lang an' drear;
How swiftly sped time's gowden rays,
    When Simmer's sang an' love were here.
Then come, sweet Spring, revive the year,
    Bring verdure to the leafless shaw,
An' bring the lass that I lo'e dear—
    The bonnie lass that's far awa'.

CAM YE OWRE THE FULTON FERRY?

I.

Cam ye owre the Fulton Ferry?
    Heard ye pipers bravely blaw?
Saw ye clansmen blythe an' merry
    In the Caledonian Ha'?
A' their siller brooches glancing,
    A' their tartan waving green,
A' their glorious mirth an' dancing,
    Were na match to bonnie Jean.

II.

Ilka lad was glow'rin at her,—
    Vow but mony ane was fain;
Pawky rogues forgot to flatter,
    Wishing Jeanie were their ain.
When she spak they stood an' wonder'd,
    As when subjects hear a queen;
Lasses too were maist dumfounder'd—
    A' the lads were after Jean.

III.

Lang they've wrought on plans for bringing
    A' the bodies to the ha';
Some would come to hear the singing,
    Some to see a friend or twa.
A' their schemes hae seen conclusion,
    They may rest content I ween;
Fowk gae thrangin by the thousan'
    Just to look at bonnie Jean.

O MARY, DO YE MIND THE DAY?

I.

O Mary, do ye mind the day
    When we were daffin on the green?
Sae sweet an' couthie's ye did say
    Your gentle heart was gien to nane.
The opening bloom o' seventeen,
    Like violet begun to blaw,
Grac'd ilka charm, when saft at een
    Ye bade me bide a year or twa.

II.

An' years hae pass'd, sweet lass, sin' syne—
    Lang years upon life's stormy sea,
But bright an' brighter aye ye shine
    The beacon light o' memory's e'e;
An' aye my thoughts flee back to thee,
    Like swallows wing'd frae far awa';
An' aye I mind ye said to me,
    "O laddie, bide a year or twa."

III.

Then, lassie, come wi' a' thy charms,
    I wat I'm wearied o' mysel';
I'll clasp thee in my longing arms,
    An' aye thegither we will dwell.
O gar my heart wi' rapture swell,
    O dinna, dinna say me na,
For brawly do ye mind yoursel'
    Ye bade me bide a year or twa.

THE LASSIE'S SONG.

I.

Now simmer cleeds the groves in green,
    An' decks the flow'ry brae;
An' fain I'd wander out at e'en,
    But out I daurna gae.
For there's a laddie down the gate
    Wha's like a ghaist to me;
An' gin I meet him air or late,
    He winna lat me be.

II.

He glow'rs like ony silly gowk,
    He ca's me heavenly fair ;
I bid him look like ither fowk,
    An' fash me sae nae mair.
I ca' him coof an' hav'rel too,
    An' frown wi' scornfu' e'e ;
But a' I say, or a' I do,
    He winna lat me be.

III.

My cousin Kate she flytes me sair,
    An' says I yet may rue ;
She rooses aye his yellow hair
    And een o' bonnie blue.
Quo' she, "If e'er ye want a man,
    Juist bid him wait a wee."
I think I'll hae to tak' her plan—
    He winna lat me be.

MARY WI' THE GOWDEN HAIR.

I.

Mary wi' the gowden hair,
  Bonnie Mary, gentle Mary ;
O but ye are sweet an' fair,
  My winsome, charming Mary.
Your een are like the starnies clear,
Your cheeks like blossoms o' the brier,
An' O your voice is sweet to hear,
  My ain, my bonnie dearie.

II.

But dearer than your bonnie face,
  Bonnie Mary, gentle Mary,
Or a' your beauty's bloom an' grace,
  My winsome, charming Mary,
Is ilka motion, void o' airt,
That lends a grace to ilka pairt,
An' captivates ilk manly heart,
  Wi' love for thee, my dearie.

III.

But Mary, lassie, tak' advice,
  Bonnie Mary, gentle Mary;
Be mair than guid, braw lass,—be wise,
  My winsome, charming Mary,
An' gie your heart to ane that's true,
Wha'll live to love nae ane but you;
An' blythe you'll be an' never rue,
  My ain, my bonnie dearie.

BONNIE NORANSIDE.

I.

When joyfu' June wi' gladsome grace
  Comes deck'd wi' blossoms fair,
An' twines round Nature's bonnie face
  Her garlands rich and rare,
How swift my fancy wings awa'
  Out owre yon foaming tide,
And fondly paints each leafy shaw
  On bonnie Noranside!

II.

O sweetly there the wild flow'rs spring
    Beside the gowany lea!
O blythely there the wild birds sing
    On ilka bush and tree!
While purple hills an' valleys green,
    Array'd in Simmer's pride,
Spread lavish to the longing een
    By bonnie Noranside.

III.

The gay laburnum waves its crest
    Abune the crystal stream;
The lily opes its snawy breast
    To catch the gowden gleam;
The stately firs their arms extend
    In shady coverts wide,
Where a' the charms o' Nature blend,
    By bonnie Noranside.

IV.

Ye Powers wha shape our varied track
    On life's uncertain sea,
As bright there comes in fancy back
    Youth's fairy scenes to me,
Sae bring me back, I fondly pray,
    To where my auld friends bide,
To spend ae lee lang simmer's day
    By bonnie Noranside.

CHARACTER SKETCHES, ETC.

TAM ANDERSON.

Tam Anderson was an apprentice loun
    Wha sair'd his time in Dundee,
The lichtsomest lads ye could meet i' the toun
    Were feint a bit blyther than he.
An' he has gaen north out-owre the hill
    To dance his New Year's reel,
An' through the deep snaw he's wander'd awa',
    For Tam was a lang-leggit chiel.

An' Tam had a lass that lived i' the North,
    An' a canty auld mither forby,
As kind an auld bodie 's e'er lived on the earth,
    An' Tam was her pride an' her joy.
An' lang they had look'd for the blythesome new year,
    An' counted the days ere they cam,
For blythe was the thought o' the joy to be brought
    Wi' the grand hame-coming o' Tam.

The crusie was lighted on Hogmanay night,
    An' hung i' the window sae clear,
An' the auld mither watch'd by the gleam o' the light
    To see gin her laddie was near.
An' the lassie that lived at the fit o' the brae,
    Her heart was gaun duntin I trow,
As she busk'd hersel' braw in her wincey an' a',
    An' her hair wi' ribbons·o' blue.

But Tam had just come to the fit o' the glen
    Whaur the yill-house stands a' alane,
An' there was sic rowth o' young women an' men
    As blythesome as ever were seen:
An' Tam being cauld wi' the frost an' the snaw,
    He ventured to look in a wee,
An' ilk ane cried, " Tam, here man tak' a dram,
    Tam Anderson, drink wi' me."

The lasses thrang'd round. for they likit Tam weel,
    A braw strappin lad was he,
Till Tam's frozen shanks grew souple 's an eel,
    An' his head grew light as a bee;
Till rantin wi' this ane, an' drinking wi' that,
    An' laughing an' dancing wi' glee,
He thought nae a hair on his mither nae mair
    Nor the lass wi' the bonnie blue e'e.

His mither sat late, his mither sat lang,
　　An' waefu' forebodings had she,—
O whaur was her laddie?—O surely some wrang
　　Had keepit him yet in Dundee.
An' the lassie she sat by the fire alane,
　　As dowie as dowie could be;
Ilk sough o' the blast sae eerie blew past,
　　But brought na the joy o' her e'e.

Sae the auld year pass'd amid frolic an' din,
　　Whaur Tam was the king o' the core:
As sune as the breath o' the new year cam in
　　The youngsters made aff to the door;
An' some wad gae here, an' some wad gae there,
　　To ca' on their neibors sae crouse,
But Tam he set aff wi' the help o' his staff
　　To seek for his mither's bit house.

But whaur he had wander'd there's nae ane can tell,
　　He paidlet through thick an' through thin;
But ere it was morning he cam to himsel'
　　Wi' a plash owre the lugs i' the linn.
His hands were a' scarted, his coat was a' spoiled
　　Wi' mony a rive an' a tear,
His teeth chatter'd grim, ye'd hae hardly kenn'd him,
　　An' the tangles hung stiff on his hair.

In this waefu' like plight like a warlock he cam
    An rapp'd at his auld mither's door;
The mither gaed running an' crying "Here's Tam!"
    An' then loot a terrible roar.
She swarf'd clean awa' as gin she was dead,
    Till Tam took her up on his knee,
An' he brought her round frae her terrible stound,
    Crying "Mither, O mither, it 's me!"

"Preserve 's!" cried the mither. "O Tam, is that you?
    O sirs! but ye 've gien me a fright;
My poor cauldrife laddie, my ain dawtie doo,
    O whaur hae ye been a' the night?
Let me lay your claes by, O Tammy, my man.
    Tak' aff your stockings an' shoon:
Lie doun for a wee, an' lat sleep close your e'e;
    O me but you 're daidlet an' dune!"

An' glad was poor Tam to get rest to his shanks,
    An' sleep to his drumlie e'e;
For wi' ranting an' drinking an' playing his pranks,
    It's unco forfouchten was he.
An' he bade his mither to wauken him up
    As sune as he'd haen a bit nap;
An' she put a het pan to his feet—poor man:
    An' he sune was as soun' as a tap.

The neebors ca'd in wi' the scraigh o' the day,
    An' speer'd if young Tammas had come:
The mither gaed cannie to whaur Tammie lay,
    But Tam was baith deaf and dumb.
She cowpit him owre, she sang in his lug,
    She kittled the soles o' his feet,
But he slept as serene as though he had been
    Streik't out in his winding sheet.

Wi' pleasure an' sport a' the kintra through,
    The auld an' the young were right keen
But Tam's mither watch'd like a sentinel true,
    While Tam never open'd his een;
Till just as the gloamin was wearing to night
    Some lads frae the neighboring toun
Ca'd in wi' a dram, an' up loupit Tam,
    Array'd in his mither's night-gown.

Dumfounder'd he glower'd like a throwither chiel,
    While ilka ane laugh'd at the sight;
Au' the piper he screwed up his drones for a reel,
    An' struck up a lilt wi' might.
Tam chirkit his teeth, an' he danc'd wi' spite,
    Au' he knockit the piper right doun;
Au' as ilka ane made for the door an' fled,
    Tam swore like an English dragoon.

How he 'greed wi' his mither, what vows had been heard
    By the lass wi' the bonnie blue e'e ;
What grand resolutions the lad had declared,
    It maks-na to you or to me.
But the truth to be learn'd frae lessons like Tam's
    Might be sung in a measure sublime :
At duty strive mair, count pleasure a snare,
    An' joys they will come in their time.

DONALD FRASER.

Ambition aften leads a chield
    To unco slips and errors,
Whaur, grim as ony battlefield,
    He meets wi' mony terrors,
An' sairly mourn the luckless fate
    That met him ere he kent it,
Forgetting that he sought sic gate,
    Nor wadna be contented.

Poor Donald, yet I mind him weel,
    That time when, bauld as Hector,
He fancied till himsel', poor chiel,
    He'd like to gie a lecture:
An' logically showed that mist
    Aft dims a sunny radiance,
An' vow'd the only thing he wiss'd
    Was juist a list'ning audience.

Now Donald was nae dosent gowk,
    Tho' juist a wee conceited,
He understood the ways o' fowk,
    An' kittle points debated.
Wi' hair unkamed an' een ablaze,
    He was a moral study:
He didna even wear his claes
    Like ony common bodie.

Some prentice louns, fu' fond o' fun,
    Soon laid their heads thegither,
To bring to light that darken'd sun—
    Nor did they halt nor swither,
But hired a ha': an' through the toun
    Wi' muckle praise they heez'd him,
An' in the papers up an' doun
    Fu' grand they adverteesed him.

An' hermit-like poor Fraser then
    Kept close within his cloister,
As kittle's ony clocking hen,
    As close as ony oyster.
Whiles through the key-hole fowk would keek
    In eager expectation,
An' see him stamp, an' hear him speak
    In fiery declamation.

Some said when rapt in lofty mood
    He utter'd awfu' sayin's,
That blanch'd the cheek, an' chill'd the blood,
    An' flegg'd the verra weans.
It looked as if he seemed to scan
    Some elemental brewin'—
Some dark wrang waft in Nature's plan,
    An' then the crash o' ruin.

Poor chield! he little kenn'd the end
    O' a' his preparation,
How first his heart gied sic a stend
    An' then took palpitation.
How choked his voice, tho', truth to tell,
    He'd chow'd some sugar-candie;
Forby he'd fortified himsel'
    Wi' twa 'r three nips o' brandy.

But deil-ma-care, as soon's he saw
    The thrang o' glow'rin faces,
His wits an' courage fled awa',
    An' terror took their places.
His chattering teeth an' trembling legs
    Were automatic wonder;
An' then a shower o' rotten eggs
    Crashed round his lugs like thunder.

In fury first he tore his hair;
    Then gaped his mou to mutter;
But some ane choked his wild despair
    Wi' half a-pound o' butter;
Then wild he sprauchled round the stage
    Like ony Jockie-blindy;
Then dash'd his head in frantic rage
    Out through the big ha' window.

Now lat ilk honest man tak' tent,
    An' heedna vain ambition;
But try an' dwall at hame content,
    An' mind his ain condition.
Should love o' glory lure ye on,
    Like Hannibal or Cæsar,
O! for a moment think upon
    The doom o' Donald Fraser.

THE DROUKIT PEDDLER.

Ken ye ought o' Wat the peddler?
    Vow, but he's a graceless vaig;
Sic a waefu' wanworth meddler
    Weel deserves a hankit craig.

Mony ane he's sair tormented,
    Driven women's heads agee,
Till their dreams wi' Wat are haunted,
    Peddling wi' his puckle tea.

Ilka ane wi' spite he stounds aye,
    Aft their doors they'll tightly lock;
Wat, regairdless, goes his rounds aye,
    Reg'lar as an aucht-day clock.

Fient the rap afore he enters,
    Slap the door gangs to the wa',
Bauldly in the villain ventures,
    Peddler, paper-pocks, an' a'.

But the foot o' rude intrusion
    Wanders whiles to sorrow's schule :
And the hand o' retribution
    Wrought the peddler muckle dule.

Jean Macraw, that carefu' creature,
    Cleans her house with fashious fyke.
Night and day—it is her nature—
    Working aye as hard 's ye like.

Now, the chairs and stools she 's drilling,
    Ben the house in raukit raw :
Now she's prappit near the ceiling,
    Straikin whitening on the wa'.

Little thought she, worthy woman—
    Busy wi' her mixture het—
O' the waefu' peddler comin',
    Or the droukin he would get.

In he bang'd, the whitening whummlet
    Wi' a sclutter owre his skull ;
Backlin's headlang doun he tummlet—
    Buller'd maist like ony bull.

Dazed was he an' fairly doitit,
    Rack'd wi' anguish o' despair,
Sprauchled up, then owre he cloitit,
    Cowpit catmaw doun the stair.

Auld an' young in tumult gather'd,
　　Jeannie danc'd an' craw'd fu' crouse,
Wives delighted, blythely blather'd,
　　Roars o' laughter shook the house.

Wat, puir chield—nane did lament him—
　　Clear'd his een and sought the road,
Aff an' never look'd ahint him,
　　Rinnin like a hunted tod.

THE INVENTOR.

A' ye wha 're to invention gien,
Wha work, like moudywarts, unseen
To bring to light some new machine—
　　Ye men o' worth,
Your handiwark 's no worth a preen
　　Frae this henceforth.

A chield has come o' wondrous sleight,
Whase cunning hand and deep insight
Dispels ilk film that dims the flight
　　O fancy's ray,
Like vapors fleeting at the light
　　O' dawning day.

I doubtna some will sneer an' snarl
To hear that ae auld-farrant carl
Has flash'd like ony pouther barrel,
    An' shown himsel'
Throughout the hale mechanic warl'
    He bears the bell.

O could you see him in his glory—
A sma' room in an upper storey—
His rev'rend pow like winter, hoary—
    His kindling een,
An' hear the deep mysterious story
    O' ilk machine.

Some work wi' bauks that shog or swing,
Some rin wi' weights that wag or hing,
Some hum like bees, some wi' a spring
    Come thuddin roun',
Some whirr like paitricks on the wing
    Wi' rattling soun'.

An' then what countless ends an' uses—
What wonner-wark ilk thing produces—
There's souters' awls an' tailors' guses
    That work their lane,
An' rams for dingin doun auld houses
    O' brick or stane.

What polish'd cranks! what grand confusion!
Like some fantastic wild illusion :
What cantrip skill! what rowth o' fusion,
             That mak's nae fyke
To hoist tons by the hunder thousan'.
             As heigh's ye like!

Forby, what wrangs his skill's been right'ning!
Nae boilers now exploding, fright'ning :
His patent streaks o' harness'd lightning
             Does a' the wark—
Our comfort and our power he's height'ning
             Out owre the mark.

O grant him soon a noble pension,
And joy beyond a' comprehension :
And may the tither new invention
             Expand his fame,
Till fowk in rapture blythely mention
             The bodie's name.

THE QUOIT-PLAYERS.

What unco chances whiles will fa'
 To ony human creature;
How, kick'd about like fortune's ba',
 We prove our fickle nature.
While ane will mourn wi' tearfu' e'e
 Some dule right unexpeckit,
Anither big wi' joy we 'll see
 As bright as ony cricket.

Ae time I mind, when joyfu' June
 Had brought the wand'ring swallows,
An' sweet ilk feather'd songster's tune
 Rang through the leafy hallows;
An' Nature wore her richest grace,
 For flow'rs and blossoms mony
Were scatter'd owre earth's smiling face,
 An' a' was blythe an' bonnie.

An' thrangin frae the neib'rin toun
　　Cam mony a cheery carl,
As crouse as claimants for a crown
　　They look'd for a' the warl'.
There mony a weel-skill'd curling skip
　　Cam wi' his quoits provided:
For there, that day, the championship
　　Was gaun to be decided.

An' motts were placed, an' pair an pair
　　They stript them for the battle,
An' sune the quoits glanc'd through the air,
　　An' rang the tither rattle.
An' sudden shouts and loud guffaws
　　Cam thick an' thrang thegither,
Confused as ony flock o' craws
　　Foreboding windy weather.

An' some keep pitching lang an' dour,
　　Weel-match'd an' teuch 's the widdie;
While ithers canna stand the stour,
　　But knuckle doun fu' ready.
An' till 't again the victor's fa'
　　Wi' keener, prouder pleasure;
While rowth o' joy swells ane an' a'
　　Wi' overflowing measure.

O manly sport in open field,
    Life-kindling recreation!
Compared wi' thee what else can yield
    Sic glowing animation?
Gin feckless fules wha idly thrang
    To city balls an' theatres,
Wad tak' to thee they 'd grow sae strang
    They 'd look like ither creatures.

But see they 've feckly dune their best,
    An' mony a pech it 's ta'en them.
Till twa are left to stand the test,
    An' fecht it out atween them :—
Twa rare auld chaps o' muckle fame,
    I wat they 're baith fu' handy :
Ane muckle Willie was by name,
    The tither siccar Sandie.

Now Sandie had an unco kind
    O' silent meditation,—
A gath'ring in o' heart an' mind,—
    A rapt deliberation ;
An' nane daur draw a breath while he
    Stood fierce as ony Pagan,
Till whizz his weel-aim'd quoit wad flee
    Like ony fiery dragon!

But Willie—open-hearted chiel—
    He never liked to face it,
Till some tried freend wad cheer him weel,
    An' tell him whaur to place it.
An' sic a job was just the thing
    That quoiters lik'd to cherish,
An' loud they gar'd the echoes ring
    Throughout the neib'rin parish.

An' sair they battled, baith as brave
    As game-cocks fechtin frantic;—
The tae shot silent as the grave,
    The tither wild 's th' Atlantic.
An' neck an' neck they ran the race,
    At ithers' heels they rattled,
Until they reach'd that kittle place—
    The shots that were to settle 't.

An' sae it was when Sandie stood
    In breathless preparation,
Some senseless gowk in frenzied mood,
    Owrecome wi' agitation,
Yell'd out—"O Sandie, steady now!
    Let 's see you play a ringer!"
Distraction rack'd puir Sandie's pow,
    An' skill forsook his finger.

Awa' the erring quoit gaed skeugh
    Wi' wildly waublin birl,
An' owre a bare pow, sure aneuch,
    It strak wi' fearfu' dirl;
A puir newspaper chield it was,
    An' aft the fowk did wyte him
For pawning that sad saul o' his
    In scraping up an "item."

But fegs, to gie the deil his due,
    For facts should ne'er be slighted,
At antrin times by chance somehow
    He gar'd the wrang be righted.
An' sae when that erratic quoit
    Maist fell'd him wi' a tummle,
Awa' it bounced wi' bev'llin skyte,
    An' on the mott played whummle.

Confusion seized baith auld an' young,
    Nae uproar could surmount it:
Some vowed the quoit was fairly flung,
    Some said they couldna count it.
The referee owned up at last
    'T was past his comprehension:
Quo' he, "Sic unco kittle cast
    Maun bide next year's Convention."

Then Willie aimed; while some ane, seized
    Wi' wildest quoiting clamor,
Cries "Willie, raise your quoit, man, raise 't,
    An' strike this like a hammer!
'T will ding auld Sandie's i' the yird.
    Ne'er let mischance defy you:
You 'll win the day yet. tak' my word.
    Gude luck will ne'er gae by you."

Encouraged. Willie wing'd his quoit
    Fair as a rocket spinning.
While ilka ane in wild delight
    Were to the far end rinnin:
When some rough chield, in reckless speed,
    Tramp'd on his neibor's corns:
When half a dozen heels owre head
    Fell like a pock o' horns.

The quoit played thud, a murd'rous yell
    Proclaimed a new disaster;
Some cried for mercy whaur they fell,
    Some cried for dacklin plaister.
Ane vowed the quoit had broke his back,
    Twa spak o' waur distresses:
Anither said he got a whack
    That crack'd a pair o' glasses.

Some gabbled loud, some laugh'd like mad:
    Nae wild discordant rabble
E'er sic supreme dominion had
    Sin' at the Tower o' Babel.
But sweet accord cam in at last,
    An' ilka honest billie
Agreed that medals should be cast
    For Sandie an' for Willie.

Like royal heroes, hame they cam
    In glorious glee thegither,
An' pledg'd their friendship owre a dram
    O' punch wi' ane anither.
But nae like kings wha seldom care
    For chields when they 've mischieved them,
They baith watch'd weel the sick an' sair,
    Till healing Time relieved them.

Lang may they thrive, while ilk ane wears
    His honors nobly earn'd;
Frae persevering pluck like theirs
    A lesson might be learn'd.
May quoiters' joys be mair an' mair,
    Unvex'd by sorrow's harrows:
Sic hearty social chaps, I swear,
    I 've never met their marrows.

THE CURLER.

Saw ye e'er a vet'ran curler
    Mourning owre a broken stane,
When the game is at the thrangest,
    Ere the hin'most shot is ta'en?"

How the past comes up before him,
    Like a gleam o' gowden light!
How the present gathers o'er him,
    Like a stormy winter's night!

Doun he sits upon his hunkers—
    Lifts the pieces ane by ane;
Mourns the day he cam to Yonkers—
    Vows he's lost a faithfu' frien'!

Doun the rink comes Davie Wallace,
    Tears o' pity in his e'e,
Vex'd an' sad his very saul is,
    Sic a waesome sight to see.

Weel he kens that throb o' anguish
    Wring the vet'ran's heart in twa;
Davie's feelings never languish—
    Davie kens we're brithers a'.

An' he speaks him kindly—"Saunders,
    Weel I wat you've fash aneuch:
But let grieving gae to Flanders—
    Keep ye aye a calmer sough.

Stanes will gang to crokonition.
    Hearts should never gang agee:
Plenty mair in fine condition—
    Come an' send them to the tee."

"Wheesht!" says Saunders. "dinna mock me—
    Cauld's the comfort that ye gie:
Mem'ries gather like to choke me
    When ye speak about the tee.

Whaur's the stane I could depend on?
    Vow my loss is hard to bear!
Stanes an' besoms I'll abandon—
    Quat the curling evermair.

Weel I mind the day I dress'd it.
    Five an'-thirty years sin' syne.
Whaur on Ailsa Craig it rested—
    Proud was I to ca' it mine.

Owre the sea. stow'd i' the bunkers.
    Carefu' aye I strave to fend,
Little thinking here at Yonkers
    I would mourn its hinder end.

Saw ye aft how ilk beginner
 Watch'd it aye wi' envious eye?
Canny aye it chipp'd the winner—
 Never fail'd to chap an' lie.

Ne'er ahint the hog-score droopin'—
 Ne'er gaed skitin past the tee;
Skips ne'er fash'd themsel's wi' soopin
 When they saw my stane an' me."

Round the ither curlers gather,
 Some lament wi' serious face;
Some insist it 's but a blether—
 Aft they 've seen a harder case.

Davie lifts the waefu' bodie,
 Leads him aff wi' canny care,
Brews a bowl o' reekin toddy,
 Bids him drown his sorrows there.

But his heart is like to brak aye,
 An' he granes the tither grane,
Gies his head the tither shake aye,
 Croons a cronach to his stane.

Sune the toddy starts him hoisin,
 Sune he grows anither chiel—
Glorious hameward reels rejoicin'
 Wi' his senses in a creel!

MAISTER YOUNG: AN ELEGY.

Oh, gruesome death, what gar'd ye harl
My auld freend to the ither warl?
Now when ye 've toom'd life's leaky barrel
          Out to the bung,
A couthy, leal, kind-hearted carle
          Was Maister Young.

Ye weel-fed boarders, ane an' a',
Like simmer show'rs let tear-draps fa';
The gong hings silent on the wa'
          That aft he rung.
Wha now will you to dinner ca'
          Like Maister Young?

He ne'er set doun nae feckless trash,
Nor soup made he—puir useless plash;
An' mooly cheese an' rotten hash
          Outside he flung;
We got the worth aye o' our cash
          Frae Maister Young.

At dinner-time when we gaed in,
Sae cheery wi' the plates he 'd rin,
An' brought us corned beef cut thin,
      An' fine sliced tongue,
Forby potatoes i' the skin—
      Wad Maister Young.

That time when Charlie hurt his knee,
He was as kind as kind could be,
Right patient and fu' tenderly
      Round him he hung:
A better freend we 'll never see
      Than Maister Young.

When ither fowk wad laugh an jeer,
An' thought that we spak braid an' queer,
He aften said he liked to hear
      Our hameowre tongue;
An' aye we likit to sit near
      Auld Maister Young.

When rows got up about the place,
An' drucken chields, that had na grace,
Wad fecht an' tear themsel's like beas',
      An' roar'd an' sung,
They cautioned when they saw the face
      O' Maister Young.

Wi' lang-tongued chields he didna mix,
Wha fash'd their heads wi' politics,
His hatred at them he did fix
                    As stiff's a rung,—
They got nae credit for their tricks
                    Frae Maister Young.

He 'd aye things right whate'er th' expense,
An' hated sham an' vain pretence,
An' though at times 't wad gie offence,
                    To truth he clung,
Regardless o' the consequence,
                    Did Maister Young.

When July comes, if I am spared,
I 'll journey to the lane kirk-yaird
Whaur low he lies, and hae 't declared
                    That ilka tongue
Can read how truth was virtue's guard
                    To Maister Young.

JOHN'S AWA': A LAMENT.

What sad disaster 's this befa'n us?
What ill wind now is this that 's blawn us?
My heart grows cauld as wintry Janus;
        Preserve us a!
Our noble Chief—our Coriolanus—
        Our John 's awa'.

As bits o' starnies show their light,
When ance the sun is out o' sight,
Sae mony a self-conceited wight
        Now crouse will craw:
There 's nane to gie their nebs a dicht
        Sin' John 's awa'.

Sae skill'd was he in ilka thing,
That when his argument he 'd bring,
A' lowse discussion sune took wing,
        As wreaths o' snaw
Evanish at the voice o' Spring—
        But John 's awa'.

And if at times puir spite was girnin,
And through the bye-laws some were kirnin,
His common-sense, like candle burnin',
      Showed clear to a'
The sterling worth that I am mournin'
      Sin' John 's awa'.

When to the games the Club would muster,
An' Yankees wi' their fan an' duster
Like bees around the ring would cluster
      In mony a raw—
He was our centre-piece—our lustre—
      But John 's awa'.

When mauchtless athletes whiles would grudge,
An' gied our Chief a sly bit nudge.
To favor them he wadna budge
      His mind a straw;
He was a siccar weel-skilled judge—
      But John 's awa'.

Sae wise was his administration,
Fu' weel I saw our situation,
An' sair I press'd his nomination,
      But he said na:
He 'd haen aneuch o' exaltation—
      Now John's awa'.

O Fortune, but you 're sair to blame,
That raised our Club to muckle fame,
Then, like ane wauken'd frae a dream,
   A change we saw ;—
We 've tint the best half o' our name
   Sin' John 's awa'.

LANG PETER.

Lang Peter was an unco loun,
  A queer catwittit creature ;
An' nought could please him up or doun,
  But rinnin to the theatre.
He bore his mither's wild tirwirrs,
  For sad an' sair it rack'd her,
To think that weel-born bairn o' hers
  Would turn a waugh play-actor.

But Peter wadna haud nor bind,
  But lived in firm adherence
That some grand chance some day would find
  His lang-look'd-for appearance ;
And whyles he gaed to sic a height
  Wi' Shakespeare's grand creations,
That fowk were deav'd baith day an' night
  Wi' skelps o' recitations.

An' sae it chanced, an orra rake
    Aft gripp'd in want's cauld clutches,
Though like a Jew, aye on the make
    In ilka thing he touches,
Had fa'n upon an unco ploy—
    Puir chield, an unco pity—
To play the drama o' "Rob Roy"
    Owreby in Brooklyn City.

Frae far an' near the show fowk cam,
    Puir hungry-looking villains,
An' some would play juist for a dram,
    An' some for twa 'r three shillings:
But Peter sought nae baser kind
    O' monetary clauses,
But offered free his heart an' mind,
    In hopes to win applauses.

And had ye seen him on that night
    When on the stage thegither,
I wat he was a gallant sight
    For marching through the heather:
Wi' tartan kilt an' braid claymore,
    An' buckles glancing rarely,
Like chieftains i' the days o' yore
    That fought for Royal Charlie.

But how can e'er my muse rehearse
 The sad, the sair misfortune,
Or paint that sight in modest verse,
 How when they raised the curtain,
A chield stood winding up the claith
 Like playing on hurdy-gurdies,
An' in rowed Peter's tartan graith,
 An' hung him by the hurdies!

A yell broke frae th' astonished crowd,
 The very sky it rent it;
Some glaiket lassies skirl'd fu' loud,
 An' ithers near-hand fainted.
Puir Peter squirmed, an' lap an' sprang,
 Just like a new-catch'd haddock,
An' kick'd his heels wi' fearfu' spang
 Amaist like ony puddock.

Some tried to free him frae his plight,
 They cam but little speed o' 't,
Ane broke the handle in his might,
 Juist when they maist had need o' 't.
A chield grown desp'rate i' the case
 Shut aff the big gas meter,
An' brought thick darkness owre the place
 An' some relief to Peter.

Daft gowk! he minds his mither now
    His stage career is ended ;
An' may ilk foolish prank, I trow,
    Thus be at first suspended.
Ye youths wha court the public e'e
    Keep back in canny clearance,
Or some disaster ye may dree
    Like Peter's first appearance.

JOCK WABSTER.

Jock Wabster, o' Girvan, cam owre here to bide,
    But he cared na for ferlies a flee ;
But to hear a' the preachers—O that was his pride.
    For an unco douce body was he.
A pillar in Zion he 'd been frae his youth,
    An' deep draughts o' doctrine he 'd quaff'd ;
An' sae schuled he 'd aye been in the real gospel truth,
    Ye 'd ne'er thought he 'd gae minister-daft.

When to Gotham he cam, preserve's what a steer!
　　Ilk Sabbath, at break o' the dawn,
He up'an' 'awa' a new preacher to hear,
　　Whaur gowpens o logic were sawn.
Three times i' the day, and aftentimes four,
　　He listen'd to clerical craft,
Till at last his een had sic an unco like glow'r.
　　You could see he was minister-daft.

To Beecher he gaed, wha vowed that the deil
　　Was nought but some auld-warld blether!
To Talmage he tramp'd, wha proved juist as weel
　　Fowk were a' gaun to Satan thegither!
Then Ormiston showed how the foreordained few
　　Were the only true heavenly graft.
Jock couldna see how a' their theories were true,
　　Although he was minister.daft.

Then Frothingham showed him—that lang-headed chap—
　　How fowk were maist gomerals a';
How priests an' how clergy juist baited a trap
　　To lead puir silly bodies awa';
How creeds an' how kirks an' a' siccan gear
　　Were as frail as an auld rotten raft.
Some fowk may dispute it, but ae thing was clear,
　　Jock Wabster was minister-daft!

Still he tramp'd an' he trudg'd, an' hearken'd an' stared,
    Till at last, on a day it befel,
He heard a Scotch ranter, wha bauldiy declared
    He had Heaven juist a' to himsel'!
Whaur he an' his half-dizzen bodies would bide
    In spite o' the deevil's wrang waft,
While the brunstane consumed a' the earth in its pride.
    No forgetting the minister-daft.

How he stampit and reeng'd amang lions an' lambs !
    An beasts wi' big horns an' a' !
An' he-goats, an' dragons, an' deevils, an' rams,
    An' cantrips cuist up in a raw !
But the upshot was this, that Jock he thought shame ;
    Now doucely he plies his ain craft,
An' on Sabbaths he reads owre the gude book at hame ;
    So he's nae langer minister-daft.

THE MATCH-MAKING LUCKIE.

I kent a Scotch wife fat an' crouse
    As ony weel-fed chuckie;
An' social mirth aft graced the house
    O' that auld, canty Luckie :
An' foul or fair, or late or air,
    In spite o' wind and weather,
This Luckie still worked wi' a will
    To bring young fowk thegither.

An' whiles 't was parties at her house,
    An' whiles 't was singing classes;
An' whiles 't was dancings blithe an' crouse
    Amang the lads an' lasses.
The blatest pair that entered there
    They never could dishearten her :
The blate and cauld grew blithe and bauld,
    An' learned to kiss their partner.

When first we met, "My lad," quo' she,
    "We've lasses braw an' plenty;
Tak' tent an' lea' yersel' wi' me,
    I'm sure you're twa an'-twenty:
An' time it is ye kenn'd what 't was
    To taste conjugal blisses—
To hae a wife to cheer your life
    Wi' rowth o' sappy kisses."

Quo' I. "Auld Luckie, bide at hame,
    An' mind your man an' bairns;
Gude faith, they say, ye might think shame
    O' some o' your concerns.
There's bonnie Sam, an' dancing Tam.
    Ye pledg'd them clever kimmers—
They see owre late their waefu' fate,
    They've baith got lazy limmers."

She stamp'd, she raised her open loof,
    She vow'd by a' that's holy,
Her happy matches aye were proof
    'Gainst care an' melancholy.
"There's some," quo' she, "that's come to me
    As thrawn as cankert littlins,
Now ye can kythe them sweet an blithe
    As ony pair o' kittlins."

She held her faith, she preach'd her creed
  Wi' apostolic ardor.
An' aye the mair that she cam speed
  She played her cards the harder.
Some scoffers thought that she was nought
  But some auld devil's-buckie;
But priests in black fu' sweetly spak
  That grand match-making Luckie.

At last. O sirs. she chang'd her craw,
  That aft had welcom'd mony:
An' now 't was " Lasses, bide awa'
  Frae my ain laddie. Johnnie:
Nor glow'r an' gape, nor set your cap
  For my wee bonnie Tammie:
The blind might see, as lang 's they 've me.
  They 'll aye bide wi' their mammie."

But Jock and Tam, as quick 's a shot.
  They settled up the matter :
They married, an' sic jades they got—
  The least that 's said the better.
Puir Luckie swat. puir Luckie grat.
  An' pale she grew, an' thinner :
An' lang she blabb'd, an' aft she sabb'd.
  Like ony startled sinner.

Now friends tak tent an' keep aloof
    Frae a' sic intermeddling,
Nae gude can come aneath ane's roof
    Wi' dancing and wi' fiddling.
An' smacks galore ahint the door,
    Whatever be their nature,
May turn as dowff as Luckie's howff,
    That auld match-making creature.

An' ye whase rosy lips are lit
    By youth's fires blithe an' bonnie.
O walk ye aye wi' tentie fit—
    Life's dubs are deep an' mony.
Your sweet desires, true love's fond fires
    Keep close as ony buckie;
An' aye bide back, nor counsel tak'
    Frae nae match-making Luckie.

TO W. B. S.: AN EPISTLE.

I 've sometimes thought, plain truth to tell,
I might sing something o' mysel';
But Modesty, that meek-faced dame.
Insists I daurna do 't for shame.
But to a friend.—a man like you—
If ye could look me through and through,
I think, for a' that you could see.
You wadna think nae less o' me,
Than aft you 've said in warmest phrase
Kind in the light o' ither days.

Yet muckle confidence I hae
To write you or to speak you sae.
I 'm tauld you 're speelin up the height
Whaur Fortune sits in glowing light,
An' deals her gifts o' gowden hue
In plenty to the favor'd few :
An' Rumor has 't we 'll shortly see
A Mayor or Congressman you 'll be.
Gude kens, if a' they-say be true.
There 's room for honest men like you:
An may Corruption's black disgrace
Aye shrink afore your manly face.
An' lang may Honor gild your name
An' honest worth expand your fame.

For me I'm juist about's you've seen
Sin' twal year now hae rowed between
Sin' first in free Columbia's land
We took ilk ither by the hand:
An' though stern Labor's high demands
Leaves little but the horny hands,
I dinna look far round to see
There's mony mair waur aff than me.
An' when the gloamin spreads her wings,
An' silence like a mantle hings,
Then Fancy paints in living light
Fond Memory's treasures rare an' bright.
An' spreads before my mental een
The bonniest blinks my days have seen:
An' Nature's charms an' social glee
Shines back in mirrored joy to me.
Or when rapt in my cosy nook
I pore owre some delightful book.
I seem to dwell in happy climes.
Fresh as immortal poets' rhymes.
An' wish nae joy in mair galore
This side o' that eternal shore.
Whaur surely some blythe nook there ll be
For sic-like Scots as you an' me.

REMARKS ON THE SCOTTISH LANGUAGE.

The Scottish language, according to the best authorities, had a common origin with the English, and in addition had a large admixture of Gothic words which never passed through the Anglo-Saxon. This Gothic element has given it a greater durability than the English ; for while the student of English literature observes how rapidly Englishmen have altered the spelling, changed the sound, and dropped many of the words of their forefathers, the Scottish people continue in a great measure the primitive language used by their ancestors in its native force and beauty.

The Scottish language has many words purely its own, some of which convey an extent and energy of meaning which can be but imperfectly expressed in English. Its rustic simplicity has been admired by the learned as possessing much of the natural beauty of the Doric dialect of the Greek ; while by its dropping of consonants and broadening the vowel sounds, it has been compared in smoothness to the Ionic. It surpasses in the description of the humorous or ludicrous, and abounds in phrases associated with social or domestic life. In lyrical composition, also, no language can supply terms of endearment with greater delicacy or tenderness, and hence the unrivalled beauty and richness of Scottish song.

These remarks are, in brief, the opinion of the best philologists on the subject of the Scottish language ; and as it may be of some importance to those who are not conversant with the proper pronunciation of the language, the following rules, which are usually attached to standard Scottish works, are subjoined, and the reader may rest assured that too much attention cannot be given to them, as much meaning and harmony is lost by their infringement.

a in Scotch words sounds like *a* in *wall*, except when forming a dipthong, or followed by an *e* mute after a single consonant.

ch initial sounds soft as in *chair*, otherwise *ch* and *gh* sounds *gh* in German.

d final after *n* is scarcely ever sounded.

ed final sounds *it* in English.

ea, ei, ie, sounds *ee* in English.

in is the general ending of the present and past participle : where *ing* is used the *g* is never sounded; *in* is a modern innovation—a corruption of the English—and is permissable to accommodate the eye to the absence of the *g* rhyme, &c.

ou and *ow* sounds *ow* in English.

oo and *ui* sounds *ou* in French : this sound is very common in Scotch : sometimes *o* single takes the French sound, as in the words *to, do,* etc.

owe sounds *ow* in English.

In every doubtful sound, the reader should prefer a broad, deliberate articulation.

GLOSSARY.

A'. all.
Aboon, above.
Ae. one.
Ahint, behind.
Ain, own.
Aith, oath.
Air, early.
Airns. irons.
Ance, once.
Ane. one.
Antrin, occasional.
Amaist, almost.
Auld, old.
Auld-farrant, old-fashioned.
Awa', away.

Ba', ball.
Ballant, ballad.
Bannin, swearing.
Bauks. beams.
Bauld, bold.

Ben. the spence or parlor.
Beuk. book.
Bickerin, running.
Bide, wait.
Billie, fellow.
Birdie, diminutive of bird.
Bizzin, buzzing.
Blate, bashful.
Blatter, to start off suddenly.
Blaw, blow.
Blether, foolish talk.
Blobs, blisters.
Bodie, person.
Brae, slope of a hill.
Braw, fine, gaily dressed.
Buckie, a sea shell, a refractory person.
Buller, a loud noise.
Burnie, a streamlet.
Busk, to dress.
Byke, a nest or habitation.

Ca', call.
Caller, fresh.
Cannie, gently.
Cantrip, a trick, a spell.
Canty, lively, cheerful.
Catmaw, topsy-turvy.
Cauld, cold.
Cauldrife, cold.
Curl, a man.
Catwittit, hairbrained.
Chafts, jaws.
Chiel, a young man.
Chirkit, grinding the teeth.
Chow, to chew.
Chuckie, a hen.
Claes, clothes.
Cleads, to clothe.
Clocking, hatching.
Clouet, to fall or sit down.
Coof, fool.
Core, company.
Couthie, kind.
Cowpit, to fall over.
Craig, the throat.
Craw, to crow.
Crokonition, destruction.
Cronach, a mournful song.
Croon, to sing.
Crouse, brisk, brave.
Cruste, a lamp.

Dacklin, sticking.
Daffin, merry.
Daft, mad.
Daurna, durst not.
Dawtie, darling.
Dearie, a sweetheart.
Deave, to annoy.
Deil, the devil.
Ding, to overcome.
Dinna, do not.
Dirl, a vibration.
Doitet, confused.
Dosent, stupid.
Dour, stubborn.
Dow, dove.
Dowff melancholy.
Dowie, sad.
Droukit, drenched.
Drucken, drunken.
Drumlie, muddy, troubled.

Dub, a standing pool.
Dumfounded, astonished.
Dune, done.
Dunlin, beating.

Een, eyes.
Eerie, timorous.

Foe, foe.
Fash, trouble.
Fashious, troublesome.
Fecht, fight.
Feckless, useless.
Feckly, mostly.
Fegs, an exclamation of surprise.
Ficnt, never.
Fit, foot.
Flaffer, flutter.
Flee, fly.
Fleg, to frighten.
Forby, besides.
Forfouchten, fatigued.
Fowk, folk.
Frae, from.
Fu', full.
Fusion, power.
Fyke, small work.

Gae, to go.
Galore, plenty.
Gang, go.
Gaun, going.
Gar, to compel.
Gate, down the gate, down the way.
Gear, goods.
Ghaist, ghost.
Gie, give.
Gin, if.
Girnin, to cry from ill humor.
Glint, glance.
Glaikit, light-headed.
Gloamin, evening.
Glower, to gaze.
Gowd, gold.
Graith, accoutrements.
Grat, cried.
Grip, to take hold of.
Gruesome, grim, causing fear.
Guffaw, burst of laughter.
Gude, good, sometimes applied to
the Supreme Being.

Ha', hall.
Hae, have.
Haen, had.
Hale, whole.
Hamcowre, rustic, homely.
Hankit, tightened.
Harl, to drag roughly.
Hind, to hold.
Haverel, a foolish person.
Het, hot.
Heeze, to raise up.
Heigh, high.
Howes, valleys.
Howff, rendezvous.
Hunkers, haunches.
Hurdies, the buttocks.

I', in.
Ilk, each.
Ilka, every.
Ither, other.

Jockie-blindy, blind-man's buff.
Jimpy, small.

Keek, to look into by stealth.
Ken, to know.
Kent, known.
Kimmer, a young woman.
Kintra, country.
Kittle, difficult.
Kittled, tickled.
Kittlin, kitten.
Kirnin, searching.
Kythe, to be manifest.

Lanely, lonely.
Lang, long.
Lang-nebbit, long-beaked.
Lap, to leap.
Laverock, the lark.
Lee-lang, live-long.
Lilts, cheerful songs.
Limmer, an opprobrious epithet applied to a young woman.
Linn, a cataract.
Lintie, the linnet.
Lo'e, love.
Loof, the open hand.

Loot, let.
Loun, applied indifferently to a young man.
Loupit, leaped.
Luckie, a designation given to an elderly woman.
Lugs, ears.

Mauchtless, helpless.
Maun, must.
Maunna, must not.
Mony, many.
Mou, the mouth.
Moudiwarts, moles.
Muckle, large.

Na, no.
Nae, no.
Neb, beak or bill.
Neuk, corner.
Nick, applied to the devil.
Nip, a small quantity of anything.

O', of.
Ony, any.
Orra, useless, supernumerary.
Owre, over.
Owreby, over at the other side.

Paidle, to stir or walk up and down.
Pawky, cunning.
Pech, the act of breathing hard.
Ploy, a frolic.
Pock, a bag.
Pow, poll.
Preen, a pin.
Puckle, a small quantity.
Puadock, a frog.

Rantin, noisy mirth.
Reekin, smoking.
Roose, to praise.
Row, to roll.
Rowth, plenty.

Sae, so.
Sair, sore, much.
Scaith, harm.
Scarted, scratched.

Sclutter, a splash as of mud.
Scraigh, scream.
Shaw, a wood.
Shog, to move from side to side.
Shoon, shoes.
Sic, such.
Siccan, such as.
Siccar, secure.
Siller, silver.
Sin', since.
Skelps, pieces.
Skeugh, to move in a slanting direction.
Skirl, to shriek.
Skreed, a detached piece.
Skyte, to slip.
Slocken, to quench the thirst.
Sma', small.
Sough, a rushing sound.
Soūter, a shoemaker.
Spang, to spring.
Spak, to speak.
Speeln, climbing.
Speer, to ask.
Spink, meadow-pinks.
Splatches, a spot as of mud
Sprauchle, to scramble.
Starnies, small stars.
Stir, stir.
Stend, to leap.
Stoor, dust.
Strain, stroking.
Strappin, tall and handsome.
Streut, stretched.
Swarf, to fall as in a fit.
Sweat, sweat.
Swither, to doubt.
Syne, then.

Tae, one.
Tangles, icicles.
Tent, care.
Teuch, tough.
Thae, these.
Thrangin, thronging.
Throwither, through each other.

Thuddin, striking.
Tint, lost.
Tirr-wirrs, habitual complaints.
Tither, the other.
Tod, the fox.
Toom, empty.
Towsie, dishevelled.
Tummle, tumble.
Tyke, an odd or strange fellow.

Unco, strange.

Vaig, a vagrant.
Verra, very.
Vow, an interjection expressive of surprise.

Wa', wall.
Wad, would.
Waefu', woful.
Weft, the woof in a web.
Wanworth, unworthy.
Wat, wet.
Waublin, unsteady action.
Wauch, low, immoral.
Wauken, awake.
Ware, &c., wizard.
Warsein, wrestling.
Wean, child.
Wee, little.
Weel, well.
Wha, who.
Whaur, where.
Whesht, hush.
Whummle, turn over.
Widie, a rope made of twigs.
Winna, will not.
Wiss, wish.
Worn awa', passed away.
Wy, flame.

Yellow-yite, yellow bunting.
Yauk, itch.
Yaukie, itchy.
Yill, ale.
Yird, earth.